THE ULTIMATE TEEN GUIDE TO GETTING INTO THE IVY LEAGUE: THE 10-STEP SYSTEM

Insider Information from an Ivy League Graduate

*Includes Notes to Parents

Courtney Malinchak

Published by
Hybrid Global Publishing
301 E 57th Street, 4th fl
New York, NY 10022

Copyright © 2017 by Courtney Malinchak

All rights reserved. No part of this book may be reproduced or transmitted in any form or by in any means, electronic or mechanical, including photocopying, recording, or by any information storage and retrieval system, without the written permission of the Publisher, except where permitted by law.

Manufactured in the United States of America, or in the United Kingdom when distributed elsewhere.

Malinchak, Courtney
The Ultimate Teen Guide to Getting into the Ivy League
    ISBN:
    Paperback: 9781938015724
    eBook: 9781938015748
Cover design by: Joe Potter
Interior design: Claudia Volkman

www.courtneymalinchak.com

ABOUT THE AUTHOR

In addition to *The Ultimate Teen Guide to Getting into the Ivy League: The 10-Step System*, Courtney Malinchak is the author of *The Ultimate Teen Guide to a Healthy Life*. She is a Health and Wellness Coach for teens and young adults worldwide to help them live their "ULTIMATE" lives. In 2015, she graduated with a Bachelor of Arts degree from Cornell University in Ithaca, New York, where she also competed full-time on the Women's Varsity Tennis Team.

As a junior tennis player, she competed in many national tournaments and was ranked Top 40 by the United States Tennis Association (USTA) Girls' 18 & Under in Florida. She played at Number 1 as a freshman for her high school Varsity Tennis Team at Pine Crest School in Fort Lauderdale, Florida. Also while in high school, she was a member of the Senior Beta Club, a National Honor Society recognizing high academic achievement and leadership, and she was an award-winning pianist for the Florida Federation of Music Clubs (FFMC). As a sophomore at Cornell University, she was a winner of the Billie Jean King USTA College Invitational at the U.S. Open Courts, beating players from Princeton University and Dartmouth College.

For more information on healthy living, speaking engagements, or coaching packages, please visit www.courtneymalinchak.com.

TABLE OF CONTENTS

Introduction: What Is the Ivy League? 7

THE 10-STEP SYSTEM

Step 1: Excel in School 21

Step 2: Achieve High Test Scores on the SAT or ACT 35

Step 3: Write an Exceptional Essay 50

Step 4: Score Valuable Recommendations 57

Step 5: Show a "Passionate Commitment" to Something 61

Step 6: Assume Leadership Positions 67

Step 7: Get Involved in Your Community 71

Step 8: Take Advantage of Your Summers 77

Step 9: Consider the "Back Doors" 81

Step 10: How to Decide: Early Action, Early Decision, or Regular Decision? 85

Bonus Chapter: Tips for Interviewing Well 89

Resources 93

Notes 95

INTRODUCTION: WHAT IS THE IVY LEAGUE?

THE IVY LEAGUE is group of eight long-established colleges and universities in the northeastern United States possessing high academic and social prestige. The eight institutions are Harvard College, Yale University, Princeton University, Columbia University, Dartmouth College, Cornell University, Brown University, and the University of Pennsylvania.

Each year they are ranked among the best universities worldwide, and they possess the largest university financial endowments in the world, which gives them the power to provide countless opportunities regarding research and academia. For instance, Harvard College has an endowment of $35.7 billion, the largest in the world according to the *Wall Street Journal* in 2017.[1] In addition, these universities are known for their strict admission policies and low admission rates, with an average of 8.57

percent admitted for the Class of 2020 and Harvard having the lowest acceptance rate at 5.33 percent.[2]

Striving for the Best

What parent, wealthy or not, doesn't want the best possible education for their kids? The prestige of the Ivies certainly has a way of getting people to do whatever it takes to get in. For instance, in 2013 a Hong Kong CEO allegedly agreed to pay the tutoring center ThinkTank $1.1 million if his son got into the top-ranked college from the *U.S. News* 2012 rankings, which at the time was a tie between Harvard and Princeton.[3] Additionally, there are countless college counseling programs, SAT/ACT prep courses, life coaches, and tutors that parents hire (whether they struggle to afford it or not) to ensure that their children have the best possible chance of achieving this goal.

What Does an Ivy League Degree Give You?

In addition to learning from some of the most renowned and accomplished professors in their fields and being immersed in an environment of students who have achieved academic and creative excellence, as a student at an Ivy League school you will gain a validation of yourself and your ideas. All too often, people are hesitant to speak their mind, express how

INTRODUCTION

they feel, and go after what they want in life. For many successful people, admission into an elite institution helped give them the confidence they needed to share their ideas, even if they were among people of different races, genders, sexual identities, or religions. Because of their burgeoning confidence and impressive credentials, they achieved the recognition, prosperity, and success they always dreamed of.

Which Ivy League Graduates Have Broken Conventional Barriers?

To provide some examples, let's look at some recent figures who overcame the traditional obstacles; many attended an Ivy League university. For instance, Sonia Sotomayor, the first Supreme Court Justice of Hispanic origin, attended both Princeton University and Yale Law School. Indra Nooyi, the first female of color to head a Fortune 500 company, PepsiCo, graduated from Yale School of Management. Barack Obama, the first African-American president of the United States, holds a degree from Columbia University and Harvard Law School. Economist Janet Yellen, who attended both Yale University and Brown University, became the first female head of the Federal Reserve in 2014. Lastly, Janet Reno, who graduated from Cornell University, was the first female United States Attorney General.

Which Ivy League Graduates Have Become Business Leaders and Innovators?

In terms of worldwide businesses, countless Ivy League alums have been founders and innovators. For example, business leaders from Cornell University include Citigroup CEO Sanford Weill ('55), Goldman Sachs Group Chairman Stephen Friedman ('59), Kraft Foods CEO Irene Rosenfeld ('80), Aetna CEO Mark Bertolini ('84), S.C. Johnson & Son CEO Fisk Johnson ('86), Verizon CEO Lowell McAdam ('76), Sprint Nexel CEO Dan Hesse ('77), Mastercard CEO Robert Selander ('72), Burger King founder James McLamore ('47), Coors Brewing Company CEO Adolph Coors ('37), Priceline.com founder Jay Walker ('77), Staples founder Myra Hart ('62), and Atkins developer Robert Atkins ('55), among others.[4]

There are also numerous Ivy Leaguers who were innovators and Nobel laureates in Chemistry, Physics, Economics, Literature, and Peace. Many have been Heads of State, U.S. Supreme Court Justices, Cabinet members, Governors, Senators, Diplomats, Judges, and Congressmen, and thousands were and remain leaders in business, medicine, anthropology, sociology, economics, psychology, philosophy, music, architecture and design, fine arts, film, journalism, and government.

Other famous names include Susan Wojcicki, the

INTRODUCTION

CEO of YouTube (Harvard College), Donald Trump (University of Pennsylvania), George W. Bush (Yale University), Bill Clinton (Yale Law School), Hillary Clinton (Yale Law School), John F. Kennedy (Harvard College), Gerald Ford (Yale Law School), Michael Bloomberg (Harvard Business School), Warren Buffett (University of Pennsylvania and Columbia Business School), and the two men who were inspired to create their empires while attending Harvard College: Mark Zuckerberg, cofounder and CEO of Facebook, and Bill Gates, the cofounder of Microsoft.

What About the Money?

In addition to the power and fame, these figures are among the most wealthy worldwide. Michael Bloomberg is worth over $47.5 billion, Mark Zuckerberg is worth over $56 billion, Warren Buffett is worth approximately $75.6 billion, and Bill Gates, the richest person on the planet, is worth over $86 billion.[5]

How Can a Student Who Aspires to Attend an Ivy League Benefit from This Information?

To determine which type of students a university will accept, we first must discover the universities' goals and objectives. Why do they exist, and what do they need? For many, *their desire is to produce the highest amount of value possible in the world.* One way they do so is by conducting research. Typically, students and faculty work together to help produce cutting-edge theories and inventions that can positively impact people worldwide.

For instance, Harvard researchers recently discovered that biological mechanisms could be controlling and managing schizophrenia.[6] This finding could generate new methods for treating the disorder, which has experienced minimal innovation in drug development over the past sixty years.[7]

Typically, Ivy League researchers take their process a step further by disseminating the information through publications and books, as well as connecting with government entities and nonprofits. Having Harvard's name tied to these discoveries helps bolster the school's renown because as the researchers' findings are shared, the school's name is spread.

Respect the Cycle

Another way elite schools create value is by educating and inspiring its students to make a name for themselves in the world. As mentioned before, Bill Gates and Mark Zuckerberg both attended Harvard. The fact that Harvard is associated with such high-caliber people automatically provides Harvard with a better reputation. This fact explains why schools publicize anything noteworthy that is accomplished by their current students or alums; it feeds into their virtuous cycle. As the university's students achieve more, the school gains a better reputation. As the school gains a better reputation, it gains more funding, and it attracts better students. As the school attracts better students, the university's students achieve more. Therefore, the cycle continuously advances, which is why the Ivy League schools will probably be the most highly regarded institutions for a long time to come.

Celebrity Status

In addition to having scholars, "geniuses," and innovators attend their institution, having well-known actors and television personalities on campus can bring more pull to a university as well. Here is a list of some of the actors, actresses, singers, hosts, and celebrities that attended (but didn't all necessarily graduate from) Ivy League institutions: Matt Damon (Harvard College), Meryl Streep (Yale University), Jake Gyllenhaal (Columbia University), Natalie Portman (Harvard College), Jane Lynch (Cornell University), Conan O'Brien (Harvard College), Emma Watson (Brown University),

James Franco (Yale University), John Krasinski (Brown University), Bill Nye (Cornell University), Edward Norton (Yale University), Claire Danes (Yale University), Rashida Jones (Harvard College), Elizabeth Banks (University of Pennsylvania), John Legend (University of Pennsylvania), Brooke Shields (Princeton University), Bill Maher (Cornell University), Liev Schreiber (Yale University), Jodie Foster (Yale University), Julie Bowen (Brown University), David Duchovny (Princeton University), Alisha Tyler (Dartmouth College), Julia Stiles (Columbia University), Christopher Reeve (Cornell University), Mindy Kaling (Dartmouth College), Anderson Cooper (Yale University), Dean Cain (Princeton University), Joseph Gordon-Levitt (Columbia University), and the list goes on.

So What Can I Do Now?

As the saying goes: "The best predictor of future success is past achievement." Therefore, to convince admissions officers you will accomplish great feats in the future, *you must accomplish great feats in high school.* This means doing something spectacular, unique, and extraordinary—something most people in your class, school, city, or even nation cannot do. Achieve the highest ranking or skill level possible.

INTRODUCTION

Ivy League admissions officers want *leaders*, not followers. They want someone who will have a direct impact on the world. Being simply "well-rounded" is not impressive because you are not excelling at one thing; you do not stand out from the crowd. Many people get stuck being a "Jack of all trades": they play an instrument, are involved in a JV sport, get good grades, volunteer countless hours at a homeless shelter, and are members of a few clubs.

Since the world has become incredibly specialized, fields are so deeply developed and competitors are so advanced that being an absolute expert at one thing is necessary to be successful. Don't be "good" at multiple things; *be "extraordinary" at one thing*.

How Do I Know What I Want to Be at Eighteen, Seventeen, or Even Fifteen?

That's the best part. You don't necessarily have to decide what you want to be or do for the rest of your life as a high school freshman. Colleges understand that your interests and passions might change as you grow older, adapt, and learn new things. In fact, they encourage you to explore your options. Today you might be a nationally ranked swimmer, and in ten years you could be performing brain surgery. Admissions officers are more focused on you *demonstrating your ability to succeed highly in something,* not necessarily in the exact area you will eventually succeed in. They know the hard work, sacrifice, commitment, drive, and dedication required for a top performer, athlete, or innovator to be successful, so whatever career path or field you decide to do later, the same characteristics will cross over and blossom into success. To set yourself apart from all the other applicants, show that you are disciplined and focused in one area; *be world-class.*

Create Your "Hook"

Find your area of interest and do something *groundbreaking* in that field. Make that your *number one focus* every single day. If you are an athlete, practice every day and compete at the national level. If you excel in computer programming, discover new codes or create an iPhone app that is rated among the Top 100 in the App Store. If you are a writer, publish a book and win national competitions. If you excel in biology, work with a local professor to conduct research, possibly making a monumental discovery.

Center Your Application around Your "Hook"

In your applications, relate most of your answers back to your "hook." Your classes, extracurriculars and awards,

INTRODUCTION

letters of recommendation, SAT/ACT, and personal statement should come together to create a story that is consistent with focusing on your top strength.

Let's use the example of an applicant named Mark. He identifies himself as a science expert, has conducted impressive research and excelled in competitions in biology, and is planning on obtaining his PhD to become a physician. So far, he has received As in the highest-level courses offered at his school: AP Biology, AP Chemistry, AP Physics C, and AP Calculus BC.

He has gotten Bs in a few English and History courses, but these details are not as important for someone like him because he still maintains a high GPA, *and he will most likely do something groundbreaking in the science field in the future.* This fact is further emphasized through his *past accomplishments* in research competitions and science teams, high scores on the Biology and Math SAT subject tests, his full-time work in research labs after school and over the summer, and his personal statement about how his interest in biology has continued to grow. Lastly, he has positive recommendations from professors and supervisors stating that he is intelligent, curious, positive, and passionate. See how it works?

It doesn't matter that Mark is not captain of the football team, a nationally ranked violinist, or the president of Student Council. He has sharpened his knowledge in science and biology, which allowed him to *develop skills, experience, and achievements that make him special and unique.*

Find Your Strength and Excel

Being great at everything is not only unnecessary—it's impossible. No one in this world excels at every single subject. There is no such thing as a perfect person or perfect application. Simply discover what you are good at and what you enjoy doing, and keep doing it. Consider academic subjects, sports, hobbies, the community, or anything that piques your interest. But THINK BIG.

In essence, this book provides you with the ten steps you need to create an application Ivy League admissions officers will want to accept—no questions asked. It provides insider tips and tricks to achieving greatness, and it is aimed to incite inspiration for you to find your own "hook" that will allow you to excel in the field of your choice.

THE 10-STEP SYSTEM

STEP 1

EXCEL IN SCHOOL

LET'S GET THE obvious one out of the way: Make it your goal to excel in school. Maintaining a high GPA in high school shows that you are a diligent a student, are dedicated to success, and will be able to handle the rigor of courses in college.

> REMEMBER: Your transcript should exhibit your passions, assets, skills, and advantages. Devote extra studying time to perfect your strengths—the subjects you want to pursue—and you should shoot to be around the top 10 percent of your graduating class.

So, how can you be a successful high school student? Let's get started.

Show a trend of advancement. Each year, increasingly challenge yourself, and take as many honors, AP, IB, and college-level courses as possible. Admissions officers want to see that you've been striving to excel and haven't just been coasting along. This is also your opportunity to showcase your strengths by taking advanced courses in subjects that spur your interest and curiosity. Doing so demonstrates your motivation and desire to be as knowledgeable, proficient, and adept as possible in your field. Furthermore, although receiving outstanding grades in advanced courses will always remain the best advantage, colleges are more impressed by an A in an advanced course than by an A+ in an easy course.

Take advantage of your academic opportunities. Another reason taking AP courses is important is that schools have access to your high school profile. This profile provides academic context: information about the curriculum your school offers, grading scale, average standardized test scores, the amount of students who graduate and where they attend college, in addition to other numbers. Therefore, if your school offers twenty-five AP courses, but you have only taken one, that is a red flag. However, if the school offers zero AP courses, admissions officers gain a better understanding of your situation and the opportunities available.

Just do it. But don't overdo it. Even if you are not particularly interested in the subject per se, you should take the most challenging classes available because the teacher of the class is likely to be passionate about the subject, and your interest may grow. However, this issue is a fine line. Don't waste time in something you absolutely know you will never pursue. Each AP class takes time away from you chasing your true passion, so don't take on the extra workload if you don't think it will pay off. Depending on what your high school offers, taking four to seven AP classes over the course of your high school career is sufficient. Anything more than eight might be overkill and jeopardize your ability to shine in your true strengths.

There are other admission-related benefits to challenging yourself. Because of the rigorous material and high-level critical thinking required, students who take more challenging courses in high school are typically more likely to score better on the SAT and ACT. The English skills, reading and writing skills, math skills, and science skills tested by these standardized tests can be developed in high school classrooms: AP English Language, AP English Literature, AP Calculus BC, AP Physics C, AP Biology, as well as English honors, Algebra II honors, Physics honors, and Biology honors. Classroom activities include learning how to analyze passages, books, or poems; learning how to write effectively with proper organization; learning how to break down math problems and how to substitute formulas; and learning how to interpret graphs and data. Essentially, the more advanced courses can delve more deeply into problems, cover more material, and as a result, better prepare the students.

> NOTE TO PARENTS: Encourage your child to get out of his or her comfort zone. That is the only way they can grow and see their true potential.

Develop strong time-management skills. Maintaining a long-term commitment to a sport or the arts while trying to stay on top of schoolwork is difficult, so make sure you know how to prioritize your time. Develop a balance between taking rigorous classes and having a meaningful involvement in extracurricular activities.

> NOTE TO PARENTS: Remind your children of their commitments. You don't want to be a "nag," but you are still their support team. Be there for them as much as you can.

Watch how much time you spend on social media. Today, there are countless phone apps, social media sites, and streams of communication teenagers can waste their time and energy on. For instance, many high school students are on Facebook, Instagram, and Snapchat throughout the day to talk with their friends, post pictures, and scroll through their newsfeeds to see what their friends have posted. Then, once they arrive home from school, their sports practice, or their extracurricular, they log onto Facebook, Instagram, and Snapchat again, and are glued to their screens for hours until they go to sleep. There are also countless video games to play, YouTube videos to watch, pictures to re-post on Tumblr and Pinterest, and celebrity tweets to read on Twitter. Be aware of how much time you are spending on these mindless activities.

Of course having friends and being social is important, but ask yourself how these sites will help you advance as a student, as an athlete, and as a person. Most of the time, the answer is probably not much. If you spend a total of four hours every day on these sites, by the end of the year, you have spent almost *1,500 hours* on social media. You probably could have created your own successful app in that amount of time! Try to be aware of how much time you spend on what are essentially distractions, and focus your time on what matters most to you.

Find your "Study Sweet Spot." Whenever you have a crucial test coming up or a large project or essay to finish, you should have a go-to location and set-up to do so.

This sweet spot can be your room, a classroom, library, bookstore, coffee shop, community center, or even the park. Make sure it's thoroughly comfortable, quiet, and inspiring so you can focus and be creative without interruption.

> NOTE TO PARENTS: Keep a quiet setting in the household as much as possible, and don't allow teens to have television sets in the bedrooms.

Listen to baroque music. To reach your full potential, bring your headphones and listen to baroque music while you study. Research has shown that baroque music "stabilizes mental, physical, and emotional rhythms . . . to attain a state of deep concentration and focus in which large amounts of content information can be processed and learned."[8] This music pulses between fifty to eighty beats per minute, which helps brain waves to focus, relax, and stimulate your mind. Try listening to Bach, Vivaldi, and Handel while you study, and you may see a difference!

Get enough sleep. To stay healthy and energized, you should aim for approximately seven to eight hours of sleep per night. However, taking four or five AP classes, participating in clubs, and practicing and competing in sports every day can take up more than twelve hours of your day, leaving you with no time to have your necessary "downtime." That's why it's important to finish your obligations first, and then relax. Don't procrastinate or give other tasks more importance than your health, schoolwork, and sports/extracurricular activities.

> NOTE TO PARENTS: Have dinner around 7:00 or 8:00 p.m. so your teens don't have a full stomach and can peacefully go to sleep. Also, if you tend to watch television at night, remind them to finish their homework before 10:00 p.m. so they can go to bed at a decent hour. Try to set a good example and create a healthy environment by going to bed early too. That way, the lights will be off and no one will be talking or making loud noises in the house.

Stay organized. Make sure you buy all the supplies you need for each class. For instance, three-ring binders are typically useful because you can effectively insert the assignments and important papers your teacher distributes, take class notes on the inserted loose-leaf paper, and organize everything with dividers. Additionally, make sure to keep your papers in chronological order to make studying for midterms and finals effortless.

NOTE TO PARENTS: Take your teens to buy the majority of school supplies after the first day of classes. Of course, if you have the list in advance, go right ahead and shop early. However, most students buy supplies before the first day of school and then have to go back to the store anyway because the teachers handed out a specific list of what they needed.

Have a calendar for important deadlines and test dates. With many pursuits comes many important dates, and remembering each of them can be difficult. To make it easier, buy a large calendar you can hang on your bedroom wall so you will be able to see it every day and make changes when necessary. Try to write down everything, from tournament dates and college application deadlines to review session times, teachers' office hours, and doctor's appointments. Regarding college applications, definitely write down deadlines for the following:

- Essays
- Forms for teachers and guidance counselors
- SAT or ACT test dates (and prep courses if applicable)
- Financial aid form deadlines (Note: these aren't the same as admissions deadlines)

- Meeting times with your teachers and guidance counselors

- Final due dates for all other documents and supplemental material

NOTE TO PARENTS: If possible, check your teens' calendar and suggest writing down anything you think is missing. Although teenagers at this age should be learning how to be more independent, everyone makes mistakes, and you don't want them to make crucial mistakes that could affect their long-term goals.

Don't skip meals. Eating a nutritious breakfast and a healthy lunch (try to stay away from the vending machines and student stores!) will keep you focused in your classes throughout the day. Some examples of a healthy breakfast are:

- Oatmeal with low-fat milk and berries
- Eggs with whole wheat toast
- Fruit smoothie with spinach or kale and protein powder
- Greek yogurt with almonds and berries
- Something nutritious to sprinkle on foods such as oatmeal, toast, smoothies, or yogurt are

organic chia seeds and flax seeds. These whole raw foods contain omega-3 fatty acids, which are essential for good health, as well as fiber, protein, antioxidants, and massive amounts of nutrients, all of which can keep you full and focused.

NOTE TO PARENTS: Be a health nut as much as possible. Buy healthy food at the grocery store, cook healthy meals at home, and give your kids extra money for the healthier lunches if necessary. It will definitely pay off for them—and you too!

Be friendly with everyone. High school is hectic enough, so try not to concern yourself with gossip, cliques, or who's friends with whom. Simply be yourself, and get into the habit of saying hello to people and talking with new classmates. If you get comfortable interacting with a diverse group of people now, you will be more likely to develop traits such as adaptability and flexibility for college and beyond.

> *"Great minds discuss ideas; average minds discuss events; small minds discuss people."*
> — ELEANOR ROOSEVELT

NOTE TO PARENTS: Encourage positive talk around the house. Consistently speak well of others, and talk about creative ideas and goals as opposed to people. Make an effort to meet together consistently as a family. If work gets in the way of dinnertime, sit down for breakfast, lunch, dessert, or even a time at night when you can all come together. You always have the power to influence your children in some way. Build relationships with them, ask them about their day, and see how you can assist and support them. Create a loving and encouraging atmosphere that will stabilize their overall well-being.

> *"All great change in America begins at the dinner table."*
> — RONALD REAGAN

Remember the "clichés." In general, it is important to remember no one is perfect, and everyone makes mistakes. If you get a C on a test, lose a football game, or embarrass yourself in front of your friends, don't be too hard on yourself. Be able to laugh at yourself. Remember what you did wrong and learn from it so you can improve for the future.

NOTE TO PARENTS: Encourage and reward accomplishments with love, attention, support, congratulations . . . and maybe a dinner out.

Be your own advocate. Calculate grades for each class on your own. Although it's rare, teachers do make mistakes when it comes to grading, whether it's a calculation error or simply a misunderstanding. Additionally, never be afraid to ask why you received a certain grade for an essay, project, or test. It shows you care.

> NOTE TO PARENTS: Despite what many believe, talking to your child's teachers can be a positive thing. It shows you are involved, the teacher can put a face to your name, and you can gain a better understanding of the class environment and requirements.

Be a problem-solver. If you aren't performing as well as you had hoped, don't immediately feel disheartened. Simply ask other students and friends how they study effectively for tests and suggest studying together. Another solution could be attending extra-help sessions before or after school if offered, or, if necessary, you can find a tutor.

> NOTE TO PARENTS: Be as flexible as possible when it comes to driving your children to school early or picking them up at a later time when they suggest attending an extra help session. It will be crucial to their success in the class.

Have fun with it. One of the best ways to memorize content is through songs, chants, poems, or even raps. Music remains a powerful mnemonic device because the added melody encourages repetition and, ultimately, memorization. Sometimes teachers have their own entertaining songs, but try to write some on your own.

> NOTE TO PARENTS: Talk to your kids about their day at school and ask them to share what they learned. It will build your relationship with them and help them learn at a quicker pace.

Keep your goal in front of you. One of the best ways to achieve a goal is to remind yourself of it every day so you keep working hard. For instance, you can put a picture of your "first choice" school on your desk at home, on the inside of your binder, or on the door of your locker. You could even tape a picture of yourself on a picture of the campus. It sounds silly, but the mind is very powerful. Your subconscious mind won't know if that was the past, present, or future, and you might be surprised at the results.

> NOTE TO PARENTS: Make a goal page or "vision board" with your son or daughter. Buy a piece of poster paper, lay magazines, photos, and pictures

of yourselves on the table, and cut and paste them onto the page. Make it fun with words, stickers, colors, and designs.

STEP 2

ACHIEVE HIGH TEST SCORES ON THE SAT OR ACT

ALONG WITH MAINTAINING a high GPA, achieving high test scores is another prerequisite to attending an Ivy League school. It provides admissions officers with another component to evaluate students, especially among those who have similar school records; it's a more clear-cut way to downsize the continually growing applicant pool.

> REMEMBER: Although each section of these tests is equally important, you should definitely excel in your area of interest.

SAT or ACT—Which One Should I Take?

Since Ivy League colleges and universities will accept either the SAT or ACT as their standardized test, which one should you take? To help you decide, let's compare the two.

Since the new SAT debuted as of March 2016, there have been changes that make it even more similar to the ACT. Now the SAT has no guessing penalty, three sections (Math, Reading, and Writing/Language), and the essay is optional. The new SAT was created to correspond more closely to the typical high school curriculum and includes more straightforward questions instead of intricate problems.

Although there are less obscure vocabulary words to memorize, there is more reading: longer passages and more word problems in the Math section. There is also the addition of Trigonometry, which makes taking the SAT during sophomore year or at the beginning of junior year more difficult. Lastly, the new SAT has a score of 1600, as opposed to the old 2400, with each of the two sections scored on a 200 to 800 scale.

The ACT and SAT are not overly distinctive. Besides the scoring, with the ACT being scored on a 1 to 36 scale, the two tests are relatively similar. For instance, the Writing/English section for both the ACT and the SAT asks students to edit a piece of writing based on logical structure, proper rhetoric, punctuation, and standard English grammar. For the Math section, both tests include Pre-Algebra concepts through basic Trigonometry, and for the Reading section, both include four long passages that require close reading and analysis. Lastly, they both have four answer choices for each question and an optional essay. Let's look at their differences side-by-side...

Differences	SAT	ACT
Time	3 hours, 50 minutes (with essay)	3 hours, 25 minutes (with essay)
Scoring	Combined score: 400-1600 (Evidence-based Reading and Writing and Math are 200-800 points each)	Combined score: 1-36 (average of English, Math, Reading, and Science, which are 1-36 points each)
Math	Calculator prohibited in one section; 12 grid-in questions (no answer choices); stronger emphasis on Algebra	Math formulas not provided; emphasis on word problems; broad range of concepts
Reading	4 long passages and 1 paired passage	4 long passages; less time per question
Science	Science questions included throughout Math and Reading and Writing sections	Science section is 40 questions with 7 passages; emphasis on charts and diagrams
Essay	50 minutes; analyze a passage and evaluate author's reasoning and rhetoric; student's opinions discouraged; scored on a 2-8 scale based on analysis, reading, and writing	30 minutes; specific topic relevant to high school students; scored on a 2-12 scale based on your ability to analyze different perspectives and develop your own

Think about your strengths and weaknesses. Many experts consider the SAT more of an aptitude test and the ACT as more of an achievement test, so if you feel more confident in your critical thinking skills as opposed to possessing a broad knowledge of many concepts, the SAT might be a better fit for you. However, if you are confident in your science skills, speed, and endurance during test taking, you might score better on the ACT.

Consider the PSAT 10 and PSAT/NMSQT. Typically high schools administer the PSAT 10 in the beginning of the sophomore year and the Preliminary SAT/National Merit Scholarship Qualifying Test (PSAT/NMSQT) in the beginning of the junior year. This test can be a solid indicator of how you will perform on the SAT. If you don't score as well as you had hoped, try to learn why you got certain questions wrong, or consider taking the ACT.

How do I become a National Merit Scholar? The PSAT/NMSQT is the opportunity for students to earn accolades and scholarships based on their performance on the test. The National Merit Scholarship Corporation (NMSC) receives all PSAT/NMSQT scores and sends the students who received high scores scholarship application materials through their high schools. These students are named semifinalists in the National Merit Scholarship Program, and if they meet the academic and conduct-related requirements to advance as finalists, they will compete for college scholarships (NMSC).

Are your abilities evenly matched? For the SAT, college admissions officers can see and evaluate how you performed in each section (Math and Reading/Writing), while the ACT is compiled into one composite score. Therefore, if you struggle in one content area but perform well in the others, your ACT score might be more impressive to admissions officers.

Consider the implications for the writing sections. The ACT essay typically asks "real world" questions, such as whether dress codes should be required in high schools or whether students should have to maintain a specific GPA to obtain their drivers' licenses. In comparison, the SAT essay prompts are usually on topics related to the arts, history, politics, technology, literature, or current events. Consider the topics you are most comfortable with. Although the issues vary somewhat regarding the ACT and SAT, similar organization and analytic tips can be applied to both tests.

Know how to write your essay. First, plan your essay. Before you start writing, read the prompt at least two times carefully to make sure you fully understand the issue, its perspectives, and the question being asked. Figure out how your ideas and analysis can form a convincing and organized written argument. Write an outline for your essay on the space provided in the test booklet. Once you've done that, start writing. Support your claims with logical reasoning and meaningful examples, and make sure you are clear, direct, and have utilized appropriate words to effectively communicate your ideas. Then leave a few minutes to review your essay for any mistakes. One of the best ways to prepare is simply to practice every type of writing: essays, stories, poems, personal journals, editorials, and so on.

How Do I Study for the SAT and ACT?

There are many ways you can prepare for these tests. Here are a few tips . . .

Use a practice book. These guides are useful because they explain the crucial grammatical and mathematical rules you need to know, demonstrated through examples. Also included are common strategies for how to approach certain critical reading, math, and essay questions. Lastly, they typically contain official practice tests, which are invaluable because they give you an accurate estimation of your real score and reveal the areas in which you need improvement. SAT and ACT practice books can be bought at bookstores or online, and sometimes they will have them at your school or local library.

Prepare online. CollegeBoard and Kaplan offer free practice tests and information on their websites, as well as paid programs that are well worth the $30 to $50 fee.

Get a tutor. Now more than ever there are tons of opportunities with tutors and professional or specialized programs. Typically, they'll meet with you once a week, giving you practice tests to take home and then reviewing the answers you missed or had trouble with. Other places offer weekend programs that last a day or two with lesson plans and stimulated test-taking. Ask your friends, school, teachers, or counselor what or who they suggest.

Practice not using a calculator. One math section in the SAT prohibits the use of a calculator, so practice doing calculations with a pencil and paper.

Take advanced math courses. Since the new SAT asks more advanced math questions, the test includes material from a larger number of courses. Therefore, being comfortable with advanced algebra, statistics, and trigonometry will give you peace and confidence during the exam.

Take advanced English courses. In general, advanced English courses prepare you to think analytically about reading passages and phrases, which will be helpful for both the ACT and SAT in terms of their essays and the critical thinking skills necessary. For instance, the SAT prompt will look familiar to students who are in AP English. It will ask for an in-depth response to a specific argument, and it will *not* ask you to write about your personal experiences.

Tips for Testing Days

Eat breakfast. Eating a well-balanced meal before the exam to keep you full and energized is extremely important. Even if you normally skip breakfast or don't feel hungry, you should definitely eat something because your brain needs the energy from food to operate efficiently. You want to focus on your test, not your hunger or physical fatigue. If you truly feel as if you cannot stomach food, make yourself a fruit and vegetable smoothie or a protein shake.

Fuel properly. Some examples of an essential breakfast are eggs and toast, oatmeal with low-fat milk and fruit, or yogurt with nuts. Eggs are probably your best bet since the protein and fat in eggs helps sustain your energy level and keeps you fuller longer. Eggs have also proven to stimulate brain function, alertness, and memory retention.

Know what foods to avoid. On the day of the exam, avoid foods containing white flour, such as cakes, muffins, or cookies; these take longer to digest. Carbohydrates alone, especially when eaten in large quantities, can make you feel heavy and lethargic. Additionally, avoiding foods high in sugar, such as chocolates, candies, or desserts, is important because these foods will give you sugar highs and lows, an instability you do not want during your four-hour exam.

Snack properly. SAT and ACT exams typically have a ten-minute break in the middle, so bring healthy snacks to help yourself stay focused. Blueberries, apples, bananas, grapes, protein bars, trail mix, almonds, or walnuts will keep your energy high and your brain alert.

Get at least seven hours of sleep. Many students try to study the night before the test in an attempt to learn additional information. Don't do this. You've been preparing for weeks, and you've done as much as you can up to this point. The night before the test, simply relax and prepare for the next day: Choose what you will wear, pack your bags with snacks, pencils, erasers, and a calculator, set your alarm, and get to bed early. It will be worth it.

Drink carefully. Unless you drink coffee regularly, do not drink coffee for the first time the day of the test in hopes it will keep you awake. Doing so will likely increase your nervousness. Essentially, try to stick with water, and do not drink sodas or drinks high in sugar. Finally, make sure you don't drink too much to the point where you'll need to go to the bathroom in the middle of a section. Know your limits.

Should I Retake the SAT or ACT?

If you don't receive a score you are happy about, consider taking the test for the second time. Both the SAT and the ACT claim that over 50 percent of students who take the test a second time improve their scores.[9] You know exactly what to expect since you've done it once already, so you can probably go into the test in a more confident, calm, and aware state.

How Can I Improve My Score the Next Time?

Through more serious and specific preparations to fill the gaps between fixing their mistakes and mastering the test, many students have increased their score the second time around. The less you've prepped for the first exam, the more likely you can improve your results. For instance, if all you did was take one practice exam before the actual test, you can make huge improvements with the proper SAT/ACT study methods. However, if you've spent months preparing, studied all the SAT/ACT books thoroughly, and met with a personal tutor every single week, it might be more difficult to accumulate more points the next time around. You will need to change your approach drastically to avoid doing the same incorrect things over and over again.

How Many Times Can I Take the Exam?

Well, the simple answer is: as many times as you want! Since 2009, the SAT has used Score Choice, so you can choose to send your highest score to the colleges you're applying to. However, not all Ivies participate in this system, so double-check the policies of the schools where you plan to apply.

For instance, as of February 2017, Cornell University requires applicants to send all SAT scores, but the same is not required for the ACT. Yale University requires students to submit all SAT scores or all ACT scores. Therefore, if you take both the SAT and the ACT, you can choose which test to send, but whichever test you pick, you have to send all of your scores from that test. University of Pennsylvania permits Score Choice, but they encourage students to submit their entire testing history for both ACT and SAT exams.

For these schools, do not take the SAT or ACT for "practice," and if you are planning to take the SAT, make sure you take the PSAT during your sophomore year to gain the necessary experience.

Brown, Columbia, Dartmouth, Harvard, and Princeton all participate in Score Choice, so you can pick your highest score out of the bunch from the SAT or ACT. Therefore, if you are applying to these schools, you can take the exams as many times as you want without any pressure. However, after around the third time, there is typically a plateau in scores. Channel your time and energy wisely.

Think about your AP Testing. Many of the AP classes you take in high school allow you to take an AP test from the College Board. While this won't necessarily improve your chances of getting into an Ivy League school, many colleges accept these scores as a three-credit class if your score is high enough. For example, if you receive a 4 or 5 in macroeconomics, you will be placed out of that introductory course and be able to begin at a higher level.

Remember to take two SAT Subject Tests. Many Ivy League colleges require two SAT Subject Tests. The College Board offers twenty Subject Tests in five different categories: history, math, science, English, and foreign languages. These exams are your opportunity to perform well in your programs of interest, whether it's premed, engineering, linguistics, or cultural studies. When considering which test you'll take, think about your academic strengths, true interests, what your current grades and test scores showcase about your abilities, and what you might like to study in college.

Prepare for tests well in advance. As a rule, you should look at the requirements of the colleges you're planning on applying to around freshman year to start planning for these tests. Sometimes you learn information in a subject that would be valuable to have fresh in your mind in tenth or eleventh grade. If you wait until the fall of your senior year to take the test, you won't be as prepared because you haven't had that goal in your mind.

STEP 3

WRITE AN EXCEPTIONAL ESSAY

YOUR ESSAY BREATHES life into the application. It is your opportunity to stand out from the other 35,000 applicants. First and foremost, make sure you have a clear purpose for each essay you write.

> REMEMBER: *How* you write the story is more important than *what* you write about. Vocabulary is not as important as organization and the inspirational aspect or "wow" factor.

You can think about an emotional time in your life and discuss how you either overcame that or how it changed you. Brainstorm with others (a parent, counselor, teacher, friend, close family member) about topics. The following are some tip for writing a great

Common Application essay.

Show how you're unique. Your best bet is to focus your admissions essay around your "hook"—a particular strength, interest, or passion. Write about something no one else can write about—make it personal. Here are some ideas:

- A difficult choice you had to make
- A failure you experienced
- How you perfected a skill
- A place that is special to you
- Your secret talent
- When you were taught a lesson by a child
- Words that incited hope
- Your first day at a new school
- Your first day at a new job
- The bravest moment of your life
- What makes your parents special
- Your racial and ethnic identity
- The story behind your name
- How you met your best friend
- What's special about your hometown
- What you would name your neighborhood
- How you enjoy spending time in nature
- The most beautiful thing you have seen
- The ugliest thing you have seen
- A museum you would like to visit

- A place you would like to live
- An embarrassing experience
- Your first time away from home
- One thing you could change about yourself
- One thing you could change about the world
- An animal you would like to be
- A superpower you would like to have
- Your favorite period of history
- How you would change someone's life
- A huge loss you've experienced
- A favorite time with your family
- If you could invent something . . .
- If you could start a charity . . .
- Your favorite gift
- Your role model
- The last time you did something nice for a stranger
- What you couldn't live without
- The best advice you ever received
- Who you would want to interview
- What inspires you
- Your passion for exercise and fitness
- What career you want to have
- A near-death experience
- A secret place

- A difficult lesson
- A communication barrier
- A summer job
- An awkward social moment
- A visitor you can't forget
- Your favorite traditions
- The day you decided to change your life
- When you lost or found something valuable
- When you were a leader
- When you showed off your competitive side
- What your personal mascot would be
- What obstacles you have overcome
- Your secret survival strategies
- Something you can't resist
- A surprising turn of events you experienced
- Your greatest discovery

Describe your interests/passions. If you write about something you are truly excited about, your excitement will jump through the paper. You will be surprised at how fast your fingers will fly on your keyboard when you delve into a subject you truly care about.

Show your character as a person and student. The topic you chose to write about, your tone, the words you use, and what you include will typically reveal your genuine character. This overall essence is how you conduct yourself on a daily basis: in the classroom, on the field, with your family, and around your friends. Maybe it's about a time or moment in your life you learned about yourself or overcame a huge challenge. Maybe it's your favorite job or some volunteer work you enjoyed. Demonstrate your personal awareness.

Show how would contribute to the campus community. Admissions officers are looking for a student who will be a positive influence on others, whether that's in the classroom, on the field, in the cafeteria, or walking down the hall. If you have been an inspiration, leader, or role model to others in the past, write about that.

Review, review, review. Read it out loud, and have at least two other people read it and give you feedback. You can ask a parent, sibling, friend, family member, guidance counselor, English teacher, or tutor. In addition to the content, ask them to review your grammar. Even the smallest typo or grammatical error can tarnish an otherwise outstanding admissions essay.

Be yourself. Write in a style and tone you are completely comfortable with. Don't try to be humorous if you're not, and don't try to be too serious if that's not your personality. Use words you feel accurately describe the situation, and never have someone else write your essay. Admissions officers read hundreds, sometimes thousands, of applications each year, so they can tell if something is "off" or insincere, especially if your English scores, interests, and grades don't evenly match up. Help them see the real you and want to get to know you better.

Don't try to list all your accomplishments in the essay. Focus on one aspect of your life that represents who you are. Don't try to write about all aspects of your life in hopes of impressing admissions officers with a list of your accomplishments. Those types of essays are not as successful because it appears as if you're trying to build a résumé rather than being genuine, open, and honest.

Keep it short. Admissions officers have tons of essays to read, and you don't want them to be bored or disinterested. If someone with fifteen years of work experience can condense their resume into one page, a seventeen-year old can write an essay in the same amount of space.

Start early. Give yourself time to brainstorm, plan, organize, write, proofread, get feedback, and review your essay. All of this takes time. Realistically you should start thinking of essay topics the summer before your senior year.

Use the correct college name. Make sure to send your essays to the proper schools. For example, don't make the mistake of sending the essay that says, "Princeton is the perfect fit for me," to Yale. It sounds silly, but it happens.

Know what NOT to include. Don't write an essay about boyfriends or girlfriends, drinking, partying, pranks, or playing video games all day. They might make for interesting reading, but these topics will not impress your audience here: college admissions officers.

Be honest. Essays are simply a chance for the college to get to know you on a deeper, more honest, and more personal level. Even if you don't have a huge "life-changing" story to tell or an extreme "near-death" type of experience, you can write something about what makes you who you are and what is truly important to you. Think about something that incites a strong emotion from you: happiness, sadness, excitement, passion, inspiration, creativity, faith, or hope. What is closest to your heart, mind, and soul?

The Personal Essay

Some schools, such as Harvard, provide an optional personal essay. In 2014, 80 percent of students accepted to Harvard chose to write the "optional" essay. This portion of the admissions process is definitely an opportunity for you to stand out. You can write about travel experiences, intellectual interests, how you hope to take advantage of your college education, or other unique experiences in your life special to you. For example, the prompt from Princeton says:

> Write about a person, event, or experience that helped you define one of your values or in some way changed how you approach the world. Please do not repeat, in full or in part, the essay you wrote for the Common Application.

How long should this be? The personal essay is typically 400-600 words and should fit onto one page. You want to get your point across, but you also want to keep admissions officers interested.

What should I include? This essay should have a completely different spin than your Common Application essay. Focus on another aspect of yourself that you are proud of, such as your regard for humanity and love for community involvement, or other subjects that pique your interest.

STEP 4

SCORE VALUABLE RECOMMENDATIONS

THE PURPOSE OF recommendations is to obtain honest appraisals of your academic or athletic performance, intellectual promise, passions, work ethic, and personality. It provides admissions counselors with insider information on how you think; what sort of questions you ask; how you interact with your peers, teachers, and coaches; how you act on a day-to-day basis, and how others perceive you.

> REMEMBER: This portion of the application is another opportunity for admissions officers to learn about your strengths and passions—but from another angle.

Pick people that know you well and can say something

specific, and give them a *minimum* of two weeks to get back to you. Here are a few examples:

Teachers can discuss a special project you did that stood out, how you worked well in collaboration with others, your superior academic achievement, participation in class, extracurricular involvements, and/or your passion for a particular field.

Coaches can discuss how you dedicated your time and effort to a sport, acted as a team player or leader, and were always on time and prepared mentally and physically for practices, conditioning, and workouts.

Previous bosses or supervisors can write about how you took initiative and worked both independently and in groups with enthusiasm and focus, your outstanding personal qualities, and their confidence in your goals and abilities.

Bring Them What They Need

To ensure these people can write effective and meaningful recommendations, it's your job to provide them with each of the following items:

SCORE VALUABLE RECOMMENDATIONS

- Your resume (to present background information)
- Assignment samples (to help them recall your past accomplishments)
- A brief synopsis of past events or interactions in which you engaged (to encourage anecdotes)
- A list of your interests and goals
- A list of colleges you will be applying to, along with each deadline and any appropriate forms
- As a thank-you, give them something nice to show your appreciation, along with a handwritten note. Here are a few ideas, but you may come up with others:
- A gift card to a coffee shop, favorite store, or restaurant
- A box of good chocolates
- A mug, hat, shirt, or sweatshirt to the college of your choice
- A gift basket of personal pampering products (lotions, candles, specialty teas)

STEP 5

SHOW A "PASSIONATE COMMITMENT" TO SOMETHING

IT IS EXTREMELY important to show your genuine interest in something; you want to demonstrate that you're not doing it just to "look good." This fact is particularly obvious when there is a drastic increase in the list of activities students perform during their junior and senior year.

> REMEMBER: When you choose something you truly enjoy doing, you will practice more, think more creatively, and be less likely to quit when you fail (which you probably will at some point). However, if you have a passion for your work, you will ultimately accomplish more because you *want* to keep going.

When you have a true passion, it doesn't feel like work, and the focus becomes less "How can I get into Harvard?" and more "I want to do something groundbreaking in this field." Getting into Harvard will just be a result of your hard work.

REMEMBER: During your freshman year of high school (or before), you should do two things:

1) Pick something and work hard until you excel at it (at the state, national, or even international level). It might be something academic-related such as math, science/biology/physics, English/writing, or engineering/computers. Or it might be a sport, or an instrument or an artistic talent.

2) Pick at least one club and plan to eventually have a leadership position in it.

From there, you can grow as you determine and create your "hook," work countless hours each week to excel in your specific area of interest, and win competitions and awards to demonstrate your hardworking character and world-class abilities.

How Involved Should I Be at My High School?

Being involved in your school community shows admissions officers the following:

SHOW A "PASSIONATE COMMITMENT" TO SOMETHING

- You can be passionate about an activity
- You are a team player and/or a leader
- You understand hard work
- You can balance your life and priorities
- You can effectively commit to something

It is also an indicator for how you will contribute to their college and how you will succeed in the future. School involvement can include any of the following:

- Sports (football, tennis, basketball, baseball, lacrosse, golf, hockey, track and field, volleyball, softball, cross country, gymnastics, cheerleading, wrestling, or swimming and diving—there's something for everyone!)
- Music (band, piano, drums, songwriting, or the choir)
- The arts (ballet, art, or theatre and drama)
- Clubs (Chess Club, Math and Science Club, Book Club, Creative Writing Club, Student Ambassadors, Film Club, Yearbook, Peer Tutors, Model United Nations, Future Business Leaders of America, Speech and Debate Club, or Student Council)

Some clubs, such as the Math Club, the Debate Team, and the Chess Team, allow you to compete with other schools, which has a higher level of involvement, intensity, and prestige. This point leads to the next important tip.

Win competitions. Ivy League universities are competitive by nature, so it only makes sense to demonstrate that role to admissions officers (and also prove it to yourself). Enter competitions that cater to your strengths and interests; the category can be anything from the sciences, research, writing, or math to singing, piano, dance, or art—anything to showcase your abilities and display how you can perform under pressure and ultimately stand out against other competitors in your league.

Compete in sports. Join a team, either at your school or off campus, and compete in as many tournaments and matches as you can to showcase your abilities. Furthermore, pay attention to numbers. In sports that have rankings, such as golf and tennis, play as many sectional and national tournaments as possible on the weekends to achieve a large number of points. In sports where statistics are recorded, such as basketball, baseball, soccer, football, hockey, and lacrosse, get as many goals, baskets, and hits as possible. Being gifted and succeeding in a sport almost occupies its own category because it can definitely push your chances over the edge for admissions. Many coaches often seek out potential athletes from their team in advance (typically around sophomore and junior year), so excelling in a sport is a sure way to gain the attention of admissions officers.

When to not choose athletics. If you are not captain of the team or a star athlete that competes successfully at the state or national level, your sports credentials will not bolster your application. In fact, it may do more harm than good if it takes time away from your true passion. Participating on a sports team typically includes daily practices and weekly matches, which can add up to hundreds of hours each year. Be smart with your time, and focus on what you do best. Of course, if you truly enjoy being a part of the team, and it doesn't take away from your studying, preparing for the SAT/ACT, perfecting your passion, and winning competitions in your area of interest, keep doing it./

This also applies to music and the arts. If you are not able to be the concertmaster of your school orchestra or section leader of your marching band, don't waste your time. Similarly, if you don't plan to have the lead role in the school play, ballet, or choir, move onto something you are better at. If you know no amount of practice or competition will bring you to the top as a leader or strong competitor, and many other people can do what you do, the hours spent on that activity are a complete waste of time in terms of strengthening your college application. Unfortunately, there is nothing impressive about being just another member of a team unless a high ranking is involved, you stand out, or you do something groundbreaking.

STEP 6

ASSUME LEADERSHIP POSITIONS

REMEMBER: having a leadership position means you are at the top of your game, you are an expert, and you are someone to listen to and be inspired by. You have a title. THINK BIG.

Be on Student Council. Run for treasurer, secretary, vice president, or president of your class; whatever piques your interest. Being on Student Council shows admissions officers you work well with others. People voted for you because they have faith, belief, and trust in you. You must have strong interpersonal skills to be able to listen to other people, ask questions, and create a sense of teamwork, as well as the ability to take action. It shows that you set concrete goals and follow the steps necessary to achieve them.

Accept a leadership position in a club. Whether it's the coordinator for the debate team, editor-in-chief for your high school yearbook, event coordinator for the glee club, or the president of chess club, do whatever you are most passionate and knowledgeable about. Of course, you will first have to gain experience, so before you can become editor-in-chief of your high school newspaper, you'll have to work as a reporter or proofreader. As a sophomore, you still have plenty of time to do the groundwork before taking on leadership roles in junior or senior year.

Be in charge of outside projects. If you want to venture out of high school, you can create your own opportunities. For instance, start your own local newspaper and become its own editor-in-chief.

"Win" awards. A lot of high schools hand out student awards and recognitions for things such as "Achievement," "Growth and Effort," "Leadership," or "Character." However, what some parents and many students do not know is that sometimes it's possible to fill out a nomination or application form by simply contacting the contest directors or the teachers in charge of nominations. Sometimes a parent can fill it out, or sometimes the student can.

Start early. Some programs and contests are so prestigious and competitive that the student must have experience or a track record *prior* to their junior year of high school. Therefore, ideally, you should start developing interest and experience in a subject beginning in ninth grade. Also, judges are more likely to bestow the award to a student who has a previous win under his or her belt because it seems more reasonable and logical, and they are less likely to be questioned by others on their decision afterward.

Be proactive. If you can't obtain the positions you want, *make them*. If you feel as if you didn't get what you deserved (editor-in-chief at your school's newspaper, for example), create your own weekly publication focused on one of your passions, whether it's a sport, hobby, or community service project. Or contact your local newspaper and see if they need any extra writers. Although you will be doing this without pay, it will provide you with many more valuable assets: experience and confidence in yourself and your abilities, a take-charge attitude, creativity, and possibly connections for the future.

STEP 7

GET INVOLVED IN YOUR COMMUNITY

VOLUNTEERING FOR COMMUNITY service is a great way to give back to your community and feel good about helping others.

REMEMBER: Volunteer in the area of your strength/passion/interest, and THINK BIG. But don't jeopardize your GPA, SAT/ACT scores, competition titles, or national rankings for an extra fifty hours of volunteering. Yes, community service is fantastic and you should do it, but prioritize your time.

Here are some ideas:

- Volunteer at an animal shelter
- Coach a youth sports team
- Tutor students who are learning English as a second language
- Telephone residents and encourage them to register to vote
- Paint a mural over graffiti
- Organize a group to sing at a nursing home
- Teach a senior friend how to use a computer or the Internet
- Help cook and/or serve a meal at a homeless shelter
- Participate in cleaning up the beach
- Do art projects with people in nursing homes
- Organize a self-defense workshop
- Clean up trash along a river or in a park
- Start a campaign to encourage walking and biking
- Start a recycling center at your school
- Help animals find a temporary home
- Collect food and supplies needed for a local zoo or animal shelter
- Create a donation for toys and clothes to a homeless shelter

- Help someone learn how to play an instrument
- Volunteer at a local community center
- Paint fences and park benches
- Adopt a billboard and use it for a public service announcement
- Help clean up after a natural disaster
- Write thank you notes to veterans
- Repair and donate toys to a local shelter
- Help train Special Olympics athletes
- Organize a puppet show for hospitalized children
- Work with the fire department on safety programs
- Volunteer to work at your library
- Organize a car wash to raise money for a cause
- Raise a Leader Dog for the blind or a service dog
- Test the health of the water in your local rivers and streams
- Volunteer at charity auctions
- Read aloud to a person who is visually impaired
- Make hygiene kits for the homeless
- Start your own nonprofit

Think of people and organizations that could use your help:

- Children (This is at the top of the list because we should want to help the younger generation become wonderful citizens: caring individuals who are responsible, self-sufficient, and creative. They will become future workers, parents, and leaders.)

- Schools

- Performing Arts & Sports

- Senior Citizens

- The homeless

- Troop support

- Neighborhood

- Environment

- Animals

- Government

- Fighting crime

- Safety

- Websites

There are also many websites you can visit to find someplace local where you can volunteer, campaign, or do community service. Some also provide scholarship programs to awarding students. Here are some to consider:

- DoSomething.org (Do Something)
- VolunTEENnation.org (VolunTEEN Nation)
- VolunteerMatch.org (Volunteer Match)
- YVC.org (Youth Volunteer Corps)

At DoSomething.org, you can even search by:

- *Cause* (animals, bullying/violence, disasters, discrimination, education, environment, health, homelessness/poverty, sex/relationships)
- *Time* (one hour or less, two to five hours, five-plus hours)
- *Type* (donate something, face-to-face, host an event, improve a space, make something, share something, start something, take a stand)

What Will This Teach You?

Being involved in your community will help you develop wonderful qualities that will build strong character.

- Caring
- Empathy
- Responsibility
- Civic-mindedness
- Mentoring

- Teaching
- Compassion
- Thoughtfulness

These qualities will then have a positive impact on your sports, academics, extracurriculars, and personal life. Volunteering will bring you peace of mind, confidence, structure, understanding, and a foundation for life.

How Can I Make This Valuable in My Application?

Be consistent and focused. Pick one issue to be involved in, instead of a variety of causes, because it emphasizes your passion and commitment to see something through.

Help others with your talents. Identify a skill you excel in and use it to help others. This can be related to sports, arts, academics, religion, cooking, mentoring, and so on.

Follow your passion. Do something you are genuinely interested in; make sure you're not just doing it to "look good." Even if admissions officers know your high school requires community service, they typically aren't too concerned if you show that your heart is in it.

STEP 8

TAKE ADVANTAGE OF YOUR SUMMERS

THREE MONTHS IS a large chunk of time, and this should not be mistaken for one long "vacation" when you're in high school. Since colleges want to know what their applicants did every summer beginning the summer before freshman year, this period should not be spent simply "hanging out" or "relaxing from the rigorous coursework at school."

Summer is the opportunity for you to challenge yourself, learn new things, go on thrilling adventures, and create memorable experiences. If used wisely, your summer can give you a major edge over other applicants. For example, summer activities can help stimulate a passion for learning, yield topics for your essay, and add impressive experiences to your resume.

REMEMBER: The more time you spend on developing your "hook," the more you will stand out to admissions officers. THINK BIG.

In essence, summer grants you the freedom to do two things: 1) explore new interests, and 2) develop advanced abilities. You should be as productive as possible, but you'll be having fun too because you can choose to do whatever piques your interest. Here are some possibilities:

- Conduct research at a university or laboratory
- Intern or "shadow" at a doctor's office or law office
- Teach a class (academics-related, dance, gym, cycling, art, tennis, golf, piano, guitar)
- Organize a marathon or walk/run to raise money for a charity
- Volunteer to do office work at a local non-profit agency or job office of your choice (doctor, dentist, law, veterinarian)
- Sharpen your abilities in a sport and compete at the state and national level
- Produce a neighborhood newspaper
- Work on a campaign for a candidate who is running for office
- Volunteer to be a museum tour guide
- Practice and perform with a local theater company

- Work as a counselor for a local summer camp or youth group
- Volunteer at a hospital or geriatric center
- Set up a web page for a non-profit agency
- Start a charity project, such as donating clothes, food, or school supplies to those who need them
- Practice an instrument and compete at the state level
- Work a paid job in your field of interest
- Take college-level classes at a local community college
- Invent something
- Write a book, play, or collection of poems

Get involved in fields you would be interested in working in after college, and think about establishing related skills and expertise in those areas. Some examples might be caregiving, teaching, animal handling, computers, technology, hospitality, creativity, ingenuity, patience, empathy, decisiveness, or professionalism. Additionally, instead of multiple activities, you should stick to one that lasts the entire summer to demonstrate your ability to commit to a project and finish strong.

Ask your parents, teachers, advisors, friends, cousins, aunts, uncles, and even your friend's parents, siblings, and cousins—essentially anyone you know who works in the field you're interested in pursuing. They might know of a mentorship program; many companies and schools offer these. You never know who might need help or who would be eager to help you.

STEP 9

CONSIDER THE "BACK DOORS"

REMEMBER: your application needs to show how you are unique and stand out in a crowd of people.

This can include:
- Your unique personality
- A unique set of skills
- Extraordinary accomplishments or inventions
- Big plans and goals for the future
- Your creativity

Consider Picking a Less Popular Major

Many universities attempt to appeal to a wide variety of students, and that means offering a wide variety of majors: astronomy, architecture, business, linguistics, women's studies, economics, government, law, biology, communications, urban planning, psychology, engineering, environmental science, public policy, and more. When choosing applicants, admissions officers have to keep this in mind to make sure this diversity remains ever-present and help their programs stay alive.

How Do I Find These "Underground Majors"?

Try researching them on your own. Or, if you are able to attend on on-campus information session, you can ask which majors have the lowest student-to-faculty ratio; you can also do this by asking about two or three options of the majors you were thinking about (for example, Public Policy, Government, and Communications). Note: Do *not* ask which department offers the best chance of admission.

Be genuinely interested in whatever you choose. If you feel as if you want that extra edge, or if your grades/test scores/essay might not be quite up to par, consider selecting another major that is less popular, but make sure you are genuinely interested in it. You should be able to show this to admissions officers through credentials—such as taking part in clubs related to it, volunteering, or taking classes at a local college near you. The possibilities are endless, and you will be able to open your mind to new areas of learning.

Find scholarships. Searching for scholarships is not fun. It's tedious and boring but necessary because money leads to opportunity and ultimately to jobs for the future. You can search locally by watching the news or reading the newspaper for scholarship award announcements, or you can ask your high school counselor, check your school's website (or other high school websites in your area) for scholarship postings.

STEP 10

HOW TO DECIDE: EARLY ACTION, EARLY DECISION, OR REGULAR DECISION?

DECIDING WHEN TO apply—Early Action (EA), Early Decision (ED), or Regular Decision (RD)—depends on how confident you are in your decision about the school. When applying early, be sure you have fully researched colleges, obtained solid test scores, and have found a strong academic, social, and geographic fit. If you need to retake the SAT, improve your GPA, finish a groundbreaking project, or are not fully committed to attending the school, Regular Decision would be the better choice for you.

Application Deadlines: Descriptions and Timelines (Common App, 2016)

Regular Decision: January 1
All Ivies (Harvard, Yale, Princeton, Cornell, University of Pennsylvania, Columbia, Brown, Dartmouth)

Restrictive Early Action (EA): November 1
Harvard, Yale, Princeton

Not binding (i.e., you do not have to commit upon receipt)

Notified of results in January or February

Early Decision (ED): November 1
Cornell, University of Pennsylvania, Columbia, Brown, Dartmouth

> Remember: Applying for Early Action/Early Decision is a smart move because it shows the college or university you are *interested*, *committed*, and *serious* about attending. Also, EA/ED acceptance rates are typically higher. However, it is important to note that many EA/ED students are legacies and athletic recruits, so they are more likely to get accepted anyway.

HOW TO DECIDE: EARLY ACTION, EARLY DECISION, OR REGULAR DECISION?

Don't wait until the last minute. Do not send in your application the night before it is due! Although they might not admit it, admissions officers will assume you're not truly interested in their school. You also don't want to run the risk of missing the deadline. Typically the schools' computers get jammed the night before because there is too much traffic from other students trying to submit their paperwork. Try to turn in your application a couple weeks in advance.

IMPORTANT TO NOTE

Once you get admitted through Early Action or Early Decision, or even Regular Decision, do not slack off! Like it or not, colleges have the right to rescind your admission for poor grades or poor behavior, and they explicitly explain this fact once you are admitted. Getting a B+ wouldn't be considered a reason to rescind admission, but a couple Cs definitely would! Also, dropping courses such as AP Physics and not taking a science could jeopardize your admittance as well, especially if it relates to your major you plan on studying. You should stick with the courses you sent in with your application and ultimately excel in those classes. Stay consistent.

BONUS CHAPTER

TIPS FOR INTERVIEWING WELL

MANY IVY LEAGUE schools offer prospective students with an alumnus for an interview. Since colleges cannot offer interviews to every applicant, these are typically optional and tend to be more informational than evaluative. Although these meetings don't typically make or break an applicant, they are part of the admissions process, and you should strive to make a favorable first impression. The following tips can also be applied to any job or internship interviews you go on in high school or during the summer.

Rehearse. Many university websites provide a list of sample interview topics or questions they ask. Have a close family member or friend conduct a mock interview with you so you can stimulate an actual interview and practice your responses in advance.

Be yourself. Although it sounds obvious, it is important to act natural. Be honest if you don't know something, have a normal conversation, and be able to laugh. At the same time, you should remain astute and respectful.

Smile. When you smile, it shows you have a positive attitude, are comfortable, and are interested in the interview; your nerves will also settle down so that you can answer questions effectively.

Dress properly. You only get one chance for that first impression, so how you present yourself is important. Your appearance is the first thing on which interviewers will base their judgment.

Show up early. Know where you're meeting, how to get there, and try to get there at least fifteen minutes early. You'll feel more relaxed and in control of the situation, and you'll show that you take the interview seriously. Bring a book to read while you wait.

Practice common etiquette. Shake the interviewer's hand firmly, look them in the eye, answer clearly, stay humble, don't use "um" or "like" too much, and be genuinely interested in the conversation.

Some Topics to Think about Before the Interview

- Your favorite classes
- Your favorite sport or extracurricular
- Your strengths and weaknesses, how they've helped you, or how you've overcome them
- Something you excel at
- Something unusual about your background
- What you think you might study
- Why you are interested in this particular college

In addition, prepare questions you will ask the interviewer about himself and the school (something that cannot be read online).

A Final Note

Yes, test scores and GPA matter. And yes, you have to impress admissions officers with your accomplishments, skills, and abilities. However, you should also be focusing your energy on your potential once you arrive on campus; show how you will fit into the university's community as an individual. Also, you don't have to be the best at every single thing. Having one specific passion and/or skill is more important than being "well-rounded" by doing multiple activities. So many students are overly concerned with being and appearing "perfect" to admissions officers that they consequently fail to display their uniqueness. Don't forget what makes you irreplaceable. You are truly special and have something unique to offer. Embrace that, and show it off.

RESOURCES

ACT. Frequently Asked Questions. Retrieved from http://www.actstudent.org/faq/more.html.

Anderson, N. Class of 2019 Admit rates: From selective to ultra-ultra-selective. 1 Apr. 2015. *The Washington Post.* Retrieved from https://www.washingtonpost.com/news/grade-point/wp/2015/04/01/class-of-2019-admit-rates-from-selective-to-ultra-ultra-selective/.

College Board. Retaking the SAT. Retrieved from http://professionals.collegeboard.com/testing/sat-reasoning/scores/retake.

Harvard Gazette, "Researchers shed new light on schizophrenia," 21 July 2014. Retrieved from http://news.harvard.edu/gazette/story/2014/07/researchers-shed-new-light-on-schizophrenia/.

Chung, J. and Lim, D., "Harvard Endowment to Lay Off Half Its Staff," *The Wall Street Journal,* 25 Jan. 2017; https://www.wsj.com/articles/harvard-to-outsource-management-of-its-35-7-billion-endowment-1485363650.

Dolan, K., "Forbes 2017 Billionaires List: Meet the Richest People on the Planet," *Forbes,* 20 Mar. 2017; https://www.forbes.com/sites/kerryadolan/2017/03/20/forbes-2017-billionaires-

list-meet-the-richest-people-on-the-planet/#49048c5162ff.
Jackson, A., "There's Going to Be a New SAT, and It Will Be Easier Than Ever," *Business Insider*, 15 Jun. 2015; http://www.businessinsider.com/the-sat-is-changing-its-format-in-2016-and-will-be-easier-2015-6.

Jackson, A. "Ivy League Admission Letters Just Went Out—Here Are the Acceptance Rates for the Class of 2020," *Business Insider*, 1 April 2016; http://www.businessinsider.com/ivy-league-acceptance-rates-for-the-class-of-2020-2016-3.

Johns Hopkins School of Education, "Music and Learning: Integrating Music in the Classroom," New horizons for learning; http://education.jhu.edu/PD/newhorizons/strategies/topics/Arts%20in%20Education/brewer.htm.

Marton, T. W. "Yale Beats Harvard, as Usual," *The Wall Street Journal*, 24 Sept. 2015; http://www.wsj.com/articles/yale-beats-harvard-as-usual-1443127399.

NMSC, National Merit Scholarship Program, National Merit Scholarship Corporation; http://www.nationalmerit.org/nmsp.php.
Picchi, A. "Harvard's Acceptance Rate Dips to Record Low," *CBS NEWS*; http://www.cbsnews.com/news/harvards-acceptance-rate-dips-to-record-low/.

Wikipedia, "List of Cornell Alumni," October 2012; https://en.wikipedia.org/wiki/List_of_Cornell_University_alumni.

NOTES

1. *Business Insider*, 2016.
2. *CBS News*, 2014.
3. Wikipedia, 2017.
4. *Forbes*, 2017.
5. *Harvard Gazette*, 2014.
6. Ibid.
7. Johns Hopkins, 1995.
8. CollegeBoard; ACT, 2016.

www.ingramcontent.com/pod-product-compliance
Lightning Source LLC
Chambersburg PA
CBHW071750080526
44588CB00013B/2201